STOP SMOKING

BEN WICKS

LONGMEADOW PRESS

Cover design by Ben Wicks
Interior design by Sandra B. Tooze & Associates

Library of Congress Cataloguing-in-Publication Data

Wicks, Ben.
     Stop smoking / by Ben Wicks.
          p.   cm.
     ISBN 0-681-41791-9
     1. Tobacco habit—Treatment.
2. Self-management (Psychology)   I. Title.
RC567.W53   1992
616.86'50651—dc20

ISBN 0-681-41791-9
Printed in Canada
Second Edition
0 9 8 7 6 5 4 3 2 1

CONTENTS

INTRODUCTION

"Oh, no, not another goody-goody telling me I should quit smoking!"

I know how you feel. I was a smoker and sure got sick of people telling me to stop. It just made matters worse.

The warnings that I'd soon meet my maker if I didn't quit made me so nervous I'd immediately light up and puff like a factory smokestack working overtime.

I realize it's not going to be easy to quit. In fact this is probably not the first time you've tried to kick the habit. It *is* tough and I'm not saying it isn't.

But think of all those former smokers who were finally able to butt out permanently. They quit and so can you.

You don't need *me* to tell you smoking is bad for your health. And it's becoming anti-social as well.

A woman smoker happened to share a non-smoking railway carriage with the great British symphony conductor, Sir Thomas Beecham. She lit a cigarette and asked, "You won't object if I smoke?" Beecham replied, "Certainly not . . . and you won't object if I'm sick?"

"I don't think you know who I am," the woman angrily pointed out. "I'm one of the railway director's wives." To which Beecham replied, "Madam, if you were the director's *only* wife, I should still be sick!"

But today's smokers aren't just subjected to scorn and ridicule. Imagine running into someone like the 70-year-old woman in Miami who was so angry with the smoker who blew smoke in her face on a bus that she whipped out a can of mace and set off after him.

Although the man escaped, the woman did manage to spray six fellow passengers with a full-face dose of the gas, sending them to hospital.

But it's not a crime to smoke and, although most how-to-quit-smoking books tend to make a smoker who refuses to quit feel like a candidate for the electric chair, this is not my aim.

Rather it is to remind you of the many facts that those who smoke are well aware of. So bear with me . . . and remember I'M ON YOUR SIDE.

The best way to quit is *cold turkey.* Use this book to prepare for the big step. But, on the other hand, don't worry if the thought of suddenly giving up your crutch turns your knees to water. In that case, keep smoking as you read it through, then use the six-week plan to reduce your smoking gradually.

However you get there, the result will be the same.

So relax and remember one simple fact. Every night when you go to sleep you're a non-smoker. Now all you have to do is make it through the days!

1 DON'T FORGET TO SAY GOODBYE

IT'S KILLING YOU — killing you like no other drug on the market!

In fact it kills more people in a single year than heroin, cocaine, AIDS and traffic accidents combined.

Every time you place a cigarette in your mouth and light it, you are drawing in a colorless thick compound

that oozes its way through your body, sticking and clinging to everything it touches.

In a nutshell, you are a junkie. Sure, the same kind of junkie that you despise. The one who craves a shot in the arm.

What's the difference? Other than the fact that the cigarette smoker is inhaling his drug, very little.

Shunned from society, the junkie finds somewhere secluded to jam a needle in his arm. Today's cigarette smokers do the same. They now huddle outside office buildings lighting up the weed that has driven them out of their workplace.

Junkies are killing themselves early. So are smokers.

Junkies are hooked on a drug. So are smokers.

But there's one thing a junkie doesn't do. He doesn't take others to the grave with him. THE SMOKER DOES. A smoker spreads his poison and destroys both his own and his family's health.

Second-hand smoke kills just as effectively as the nicotine being sucked into the lungs of the smoker.

Would you ever consider sticking a needle in your child's arm for kicks? Or why not just jam a cigarette in your baby's mouth so that he or she can get the same kick you're getting? Then how do you feel about puffing a cloud of poison into the air your child breathes?

So why do you do it?

Why are you killing yourself and those you love in order to satisfy such a stupid and filthy habit? To find the answer to this we need to take a closer look at the monster.

2 INTO THE VALLEY OF DEATH

It was Sir Walter Raleigh's fault. He landed on the shores of Virginia and was anxious to make friends with a group of resentful Indians. He agreed to sit down and join them in lighting a piece of weed and sticking it in his mouth.

The taste was *awful.*

Rather than appear rude to his hosts,he agreed to take a bundle of these leaves to his Queen. The rest, as they say, is history.

Unfortunately dear old Sir Walter over-looked one important factor. The poison he dumped in the Queen's lap has delivered more deaths and unhappiness than any single product in the history of man.

Now *force* yourself to confront the following health facts. I know it's boring stuff, but you've *got* to read it — you've got to *face facts* :

* Tobacco kills at least *three million people* per year worldwide.
* Smoking causes about 90% of lung-cancer deaths, 30% of all cancers, 80% of chronic bronchitis and emphysema and 25% of heart disease and stroke deaths.

* Smokers have a 70% greater chance of dying from heart disease than non-smokers.

* If you smoke two or more packs of cigarettes a day, your mortality rate is 200% higher than a non-smoker.

* Smoking can cause impotence in men.

* Smokers tend to carry more body fat around their waists, which increases their risk of diabetes and heart disease.

* Post-menopausal women who smoke have a greater risk of osteoporosis.

* Smoking may damage sperm and increases a father's risk of having children with brain cancer and leukemia.
* Nicotine can depress brain activity.
* Heavy smokers reduce their lifespan by *six years*.
* Smoking is a principal risk factor in arteriosclerosis, which causes angina, myocardial infarction, intermittent claudication of the legs and gangrene.
* Smoking can increase your risk of peptic ulcers.
* Smoking can increase the risk of strokes, particularly in women.
* Diabetics who smoke increase their risk of kidney disease.
* Drivers who smoke are 50% more likely to have an accident than those who don't.

* Smoking increases your risk of cancers of the mouth, larynx, esophagus, pharynx, bladder and pancreas.

Okay, now you have the facts. If this were any substance other than tobacco, wouldn't you shun it as a poison?

YOU ARE NOT INVINCIBLE. These statistics are made up of people just like *you!*

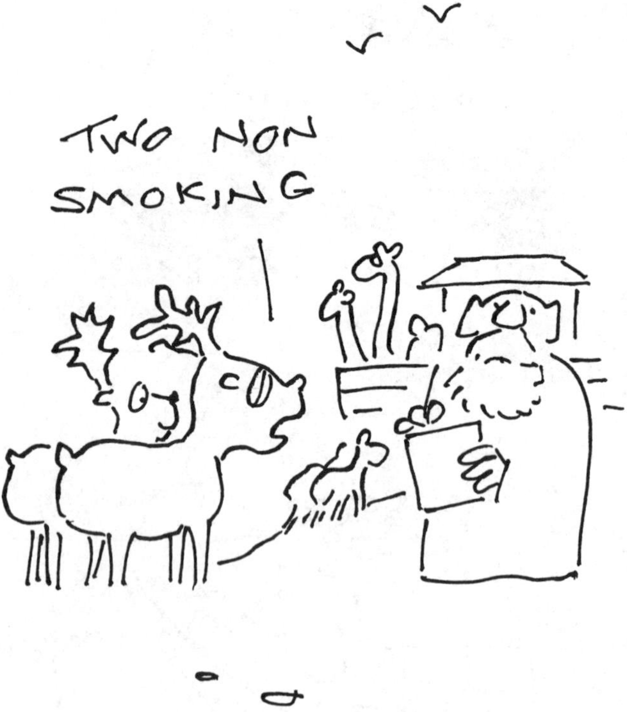
TWO NON
SMOKING

3 A DISCRIM-INATING DRUG

Nicotine is a sex discriminator.

If you're a woman, smoking is *even worse* for you than for a man!

The truth is that a woman's risk of LUNG DETERIORATION from smoking is greater than a man's. And that deadly smoke does its damage *faster* in women.

Some women think that smoking makes them look more equal to men. ALL IT DOES IS MAKE THEM DIE LIKE MEN.

The tobacco industry portrays active, successful women in its ads. It's a lie. Real-life liberated women wouldn't be *caught dead* giving up their health and freedom to cigarettes.

Yet the tobacco barons are winning their war against women. And they're not taking prisoners. The rate of LUNG CANCER among women in the last 20 years has increased five fold. *Four out of five* of those cases were a result of smoking.

For women under the age of 50, the risk of HEART ATTACK for those who smoke is *ten times higher* than for those who don't.

Women smokers who take birth-control pills are *up to 39 times* more likely to have heart attacks than non-smokers.

Women smokers also have *ten times* the risk of suffering a particularly lethal type of STROKE which frequently causes death or severe disability.

For pregnant women the dangers are even more tragic. *Your smoke is damaging your baby as well!* As a loving, caring mother how can you risk the health of your precious child?

If you smoke during pregnancy, the growth of your unborn baby will be slower and may lead to a low birth weight. You will also risk the chance of a *stillbirth* or the *death* of your baby soon after birth.

COUGH!

A breast-feeding mother who smokes passes those poisons directly to her infant. The nicotine affects her baby's central nervous system. In fact, this infant will suffer *the equivalent of smoking two cigarettes per day!*

Post-menopausal women who smoke LOSE MORE BONE MASS than non-smokers of the same age. Those smokers also have a greater risk of OSTEOPOROSIS — the brittle-bone disease that cripples so many older women.

So, women, let's get with it! SMOKING IS ESPECIALLY LETHAL FOR YOU. *Butt out and save your own lives and those of your children!*

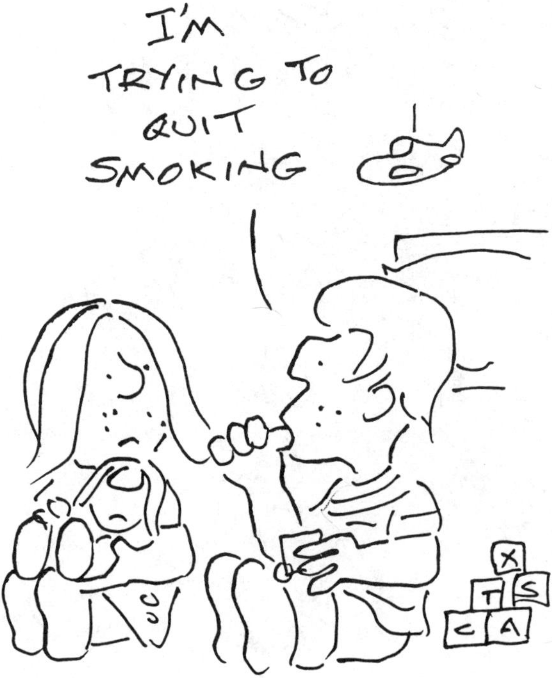

I'M TRYING TO QUIT SMOKING
X
T S
C A

4 KILLING THE ONES YOU LOVE

Okay, you know what smoking does to *you*. Let's look at what it does to those around you.

Did you know that the smoke you exhale contains *even higher* amounts of cancer-causing substances than the smoke you breathe into your lungs? You're a real danger to anyone unlucky enough to get within breathing distance of you!

In the U.S. alone, 53,000 people die each year as a result of inhaling second-hand smoke — almost as many Americans as were killed in the entire Vietnam War!

About 20% of the populace has a serious medical condition — like asthma, emphysema, heart disease or angina. Are you, a smoker, trying to put them out of their misery by sending them to an early grave? If so, you're doing a good job.

In fact, a non-smoker exposed to second-hand smoke for 20 years might as well have smoked *ten cigarettes a day* during that time. The lethal effects are the same!

No wonder the U.S. Environmental Protection Agency has classified second-hand smoke as one of the most dangerous cancer-causing substances— along with asbestos and radon.

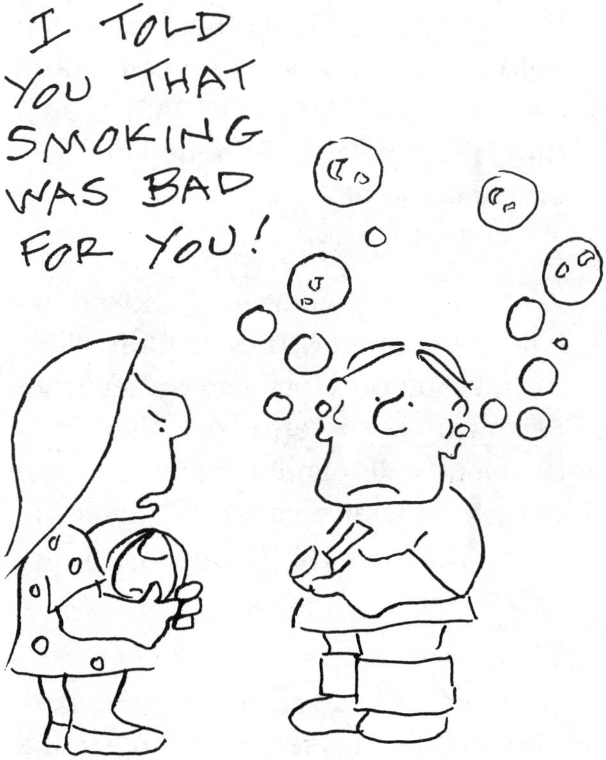
I TOLD YOU THAT SMOKING WAS BAD FOR YOU!

How do you feel about the non-smokers you live with? Make the most of the time you have left together. With your help they are about *30 percent* more likely to die of HEART DISEASE than if they didn't have to breathe your second-hand smoke.

What happens when non-smokers inhale your smoke? They're more likely to have blood clots and suffer from narrowing of the arteries. Also, their red blood cells cannot deliver as much oxygen to vital organs, including the heart. What does all this mean? HEART ATTACKS!

There's more bad news. Non-smokers who breathe in second-hand smoke have up to a *3.4 times greater* chance of getting LUNG CANCER than those not exposed.

And what are you doing to unborn babies? Non-smoking pregnant women who are exposed to second-hand smoke may give birth to babies with lower intelligence and achievement levels.

Children who grow up with smoking parents suffer from a much higher incidence of RESPIRATORY PROBLEMS. This means that your child will have more colds and flu, as well as reduced lung capacity. It also leads to bronchitis, asthma and pneumonia. A child who lives with a parent who smokes no more than half a pack a day has *twice* the risk of developing asthma.

In fact, a Maryland court found the parents

of a severely asthmatic child guilty of child abuse because they continued to smoke around him.

Every time you smoke near your child just remember this — you are making him *three or four* times more likely to develop a serious infectious disease which will require hospitalization.

Those who live with a family member who smokes have nicotine levels in their system which are equivalent to smoking *three cigarettes a day*. In New York state, whether or not a parent smokes can be considered in child-custody cases.

But there is even another danger to your child. Every time you smoke think about the example you're setting. Your child will be more likely than others to be a teenage smoker. After all, nicotine has *appeared* to be a crutch for *you*.

Do you have a loaded gun in your house? Then why do you have cigarettes?

Parents have a responsibility to protect their kids. But do these parents really love their children?

Instead they make their homes into modern gas chambers and fill them with toxic fumes.

THINK ABOUT WHAT YOU'RE DOING TO THOSE YOU LOVE.

Butt out, save your life — *and* the lives of your family.

5 IN THE BEGINNING

So how did you get yourself into this mess?

You probably started smoking when you were young — you may *still* be young!

Why did you start? For one thing, everybody else was doing it.

You'd be at a party — it was cool to smoke. At school or on the job — let's look calm and collected. Having a coffee — how better to recharge yourself? Watching television — what a great way to relax.

Wherever you seemed to be . . . out would come those cigarettes.

Whatever the situation, cigarettes were portrayed as an enhancement to what you were doing . . . smoking was enjoyable, an entertainment on its own.

Boys wanted to look tough like their Hollywood role models. But they only remembered their movie heroes as beating the bad guy and getting the girl. They didn't see Humphrey Bogart, Steve McQueen and John Wayne as they lay dying of cancer — where was their glamor then?

For young women, too, the sophisticate of earlier generations was often portrayed in movies and advertisements elegantly inhaling the killer weed. It was seen as sexy and alluring.

No more. Today's smart women know that smoking causes premature wrinkles, a poor complexion, stained teeth and fingers, bad breath and serious illness — hardly the image of an irresistible temptress!

Smoking has gone the way of the six-shooters and the corset. Get with the *really* cool crowd and BUTT OUT!

AND WHEN I ASK, 'DO YOU SMOKE?' THE ANSWER HAD BETTER BE 'YES!'

6 SMOKE AND MIRRORS

Need more incentives to really *want* to quit smoking?

How about the fact that you're being *brainwashed* by advertisers and *ripped off* by tobacco companies?

Feeling lonely or unsure of yourself? Just look at the slick cigarette ads and envy the lives portrayed by those smokers — surrounded by attractive friends, confident and having a ball. Wouldn't you just love to step into their shoes? Perhaps a cigarette is the next best thing. WRONG!

You're smarter than that! Don't fall into the trap that's been cleverly laid by unscrupulous, well-paid ad executives. Why let someone deceive you when you know the facts? YOU control your life ... don't be a sucker.

Tobacco companies live off the miseries of others. Do you want to perpetuate their incredible success story?

You see them everywhere. Tobacco companies sponsor sports events, concerts, dancing, theater and almost any other kind of cultural event you can think of. Why?

They want to look like generous corporate citizens who genuinely care about enriching people's lives.

But what they're *really* doing is peddling their drug to the unsuspecting.

The father of a friend refused to give up his two-pack-a-day habit. "Listen, I enjoy smoking and nothing is going to stop me." Then he watched a TV interview with a tobacco executive. He was so shocked at the obvious dishonesty of the man that he immediately threw out every cigarette in the house and never smoked again.

"If I'd have known I was being sold a bill of goods by a con artist I'd have quit years ago," he said.

He was right. You're dealing with the most cunning snake-oil salesmen that ever pitched a product.

Tobacco companies want you to equate smoking with achievement, success and the beautiful life. The truth is cigarettes *take away your life!*

Sports heroes wouldn't throw away their health by smoking. What ballet dancer would jeopardize her fitness? And only an actor who didn't care about his health or appearance would take a chance on smoking. *Real* success means NOT SMOKING.

Think of it this way. If a candy bar or can of pop had a label warning that this product causes cancer, would you even buy it once? *Of course not! But you*

keep the tobacco industry flourish-
ing by not just flouting the warnings
once *but every single time you light
up!*

Why not keep all that money for yourself? You could plan a vacation or treat
yourself to a new wardrobe with all that
you save by not smoking. Do you really
want to keep giving the tobacco companies your hard-earned money in ex-
change for smoke?

And then there's the government. *Most*
people want to pay *less* in taxes. But
look at you. In the U.S. a quarter of the
cost of a pack of cigarettes goes right
to the government in taxes! In other
Western countries you pay as much as
75%! You're not even getting fair value
for all you spend on a pack of cigarettes.

Why not put a stop to the deceptive promises, high prices and brainwashing right now? Choose your *own* life, not one programed for you by profit-seeking corporations.

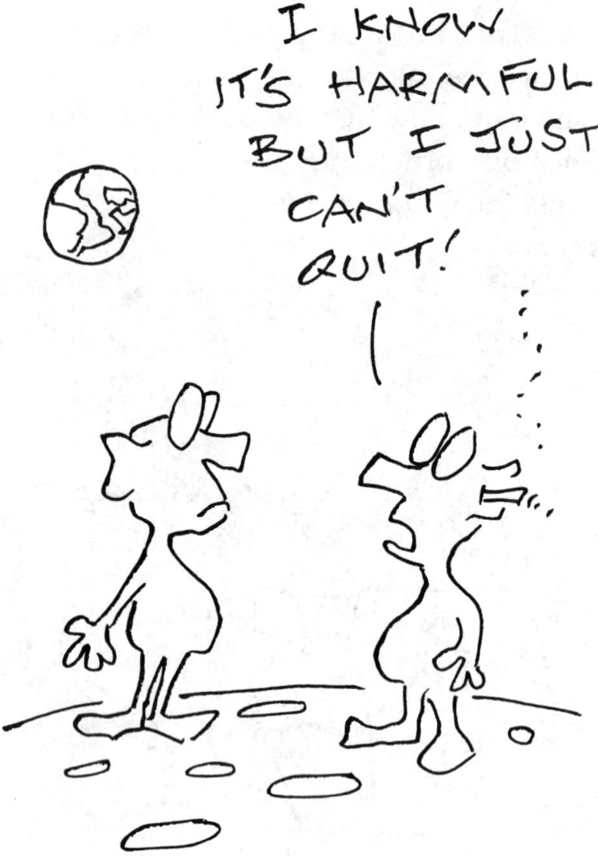
I KNOW IT'S HARMFUL BUT I JUST CAN'T QUIT!

7 "JUST FOR THE TASTE OF IT"

Okay, you know you really *should* stop smoking and by this point, even more important, you really *want* to quit.

Look at it this way — every time you stub out a cigarette *you've stopped smoking*. The trick is HOW TO STOP LIGHTING ANOTHER ONE.

So, what's stopping you from stopping?

All smokers have a set of excuses that

stand in their way to a healthier life. Which of these apply to you?

I need cigarettes to help me relax.
I'm sorry, this doesn't wash. Nicotine does *not* relieve the body of stress; it makes you even *more* edgy and tense. Most ex-smokers feel much less nervous just a few weeks after quitting.

If I quit I'll put on weight.
The fact is that only a small number of people who quit smoking gain a significant amount of weight. Most of these use the time they would have spent smoking visiting the fridge.

I don't have enough will-power.
If you can get out of bed on a cold wet morning to go to work, you've got the will-power.

What will I do with my hands?
You'll do what every other non-smoker
does — forget about them.

Some smokers live to a ripe old age.

Yes, *some* smokers do. Yet do you ever think why it's considered news? Because it's so rare. Think instead about the thousands of smokers who never even make it to retirement. The facts are that most people who smoke are cutting their time on this earth every time they light a cigarette.

I need a cigarette to appear calm and confident.

That may have worked in the old days, but today you just look out of date and dependent.

Smoking helps me combat frustration.

Nicotine causes distress, which will hardly *help* you deal with the frustrations and annoyances of modern life.

I need to smoke to get me going in the morning.

Smoking impairs your breathing and the nicotine causes depressed brain activity. Hardly a recipe for get-up-and-go.

I enjoy the taste of cigarettes.
You only *think* you like the taste because you're addicted to them. Try to remember how awful they tasted when you *first* smoked — that's the way they *really* taste.

Low-tar, low-nicotine cigarettes are safe to smoke.
Wrong! They contain dangerous substances. Your carbon monoxide intake may increase with these cigarettes. And many people who smoke them inhale more often and more deeply to maintain the same nicotine level.

Cigarettes are an integral part of my life.
All smoking does is create *negatives* in your life. It's killing you and those you live with. It's expensive, dirty and unsocial.

Take another look at your life. Since when did drug addiction lead to health and happiness?

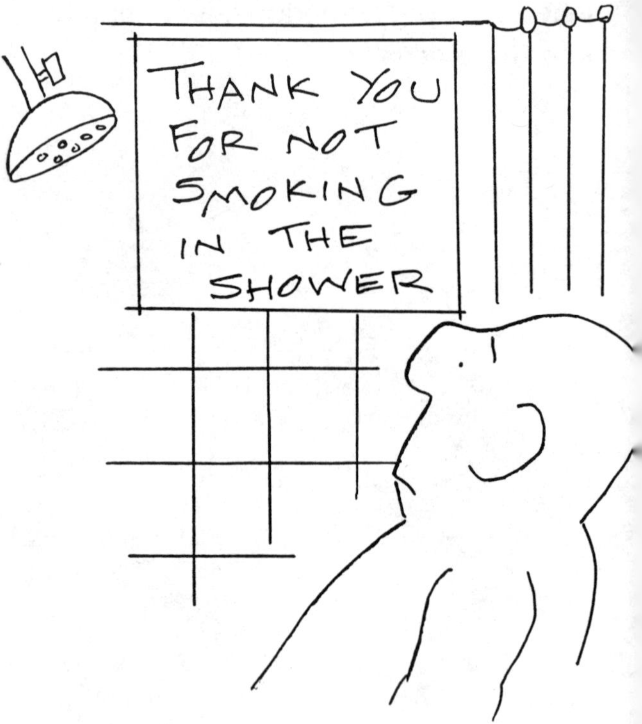
THANK YOU FOR NOT SMOKING IN THE SHOWER

8 STOP AND SMELL THE ROSES

You're about to begin a new life.

I started out by telling you that you're no better than a junkie. You are a DRUG ADDICT, addicted to one of the most addictive drugs in the world — nicotine.

Now you know the truth, let's do something about it. You're ready to begin to quit smoking.

What's it going to be like?

Unlike the junkie who shoots up heroin, you are not going to be writhing on the floor, begging your friend, who has tied you to the bed, for a shot.

THERE WILL BE LITTLE OR NO WITH-DRAWAL PANGS. What you *will* feel is a sense of achievement.

"I've done it!" you'll say to yourself. But not having had a cigarette in your mouth for a week or two will hardly warrant your throwing open the window to cry to the world, "I've quit smoking!" THERE'S THE REST OF YOUR LIFE TO GO.

YOU LOOK GREAT!

The great thing to remember is that if you continue to be a non-smoker the *rest of your life* is going to be a lot longer than if you don't.

BEFORE

But more than that you'll know how an *unaddicted* person feels — and you'll be pleasantly surprised. Think of it as GAINING SOMETHING POSITIVE, not giving something up.

Within *12 hours* of quitting you will already be reaping the rewards:

* the level of carbon monoxide in your body goes down
* the nicotine level in your body decreases
* your heart and lungs begin to repair themselves

AFTER

As your body continues to heal itself, you will experience these benefits *within days* of quitting:

* a new sense of freedom
* you'll smell better
* your smoker's breath will be gone
* no more stained fingers and teeth
* your smoker's hack will disappear
* you'll feel healthier
* you'll breathe easier
* and you'll have more money to spend on other things!

ALL THIS WITHIN DAYS OF QUITTING. It's true. *You truly will be able to smell the roses!*

The recovery time for the body without nicotine is incredibly short. Before you know it, you'll feel like a new person — one who has a lot more energy and good health.

The moment you butt out that last cigarette is the moment that your body begins to repair itself of the damage you've done to it.

You will not suffer from as much pain or disease as a smoker, you'll live longer, your cough will disappear, you'll get fewer colds and infections and you'll no longer be enslaved to a destructive habit!

Think to the future. After you've quit smoking for a *year*, your chances of having a heart attack are almost as low as someone who has never smoked!

When you've been a non-smoker for *five to ten* years, your risk of lung cancer is about the same as someone who has never smoked!

And when you've quit the habit for *over ten years*, you can count on living almost as long as someone who has never smoked!

9 TAKE YOUR FINGER OFF THE TRIGGER

Your addiction involves more than just your need for nicotine. It's a *double addiction*. The other half is the PSYCHO-LOGICAL ADDICTION.

That's the part that tells you it's time to light up when you begin a phone call, have a cup of coffee or finish a meal — whether or not it's time for your next nicotine fix.

You will find that there are certain situations and behaviors that *trigger* you to smoke *all on their own*.

There's no point in *only* fighting your nicotine addiction. That's a recipe for failure. In order to defeat *both aspects* of your addiction you'll have to be on guard for the PSYCHOLOGICAL part.

The first step is to identify what these TRIGGER SITUATIONS are. We must know the enemy in order to fight it.

Here is a checklist. Take a look and tick off the ones that relate to you.

Do you smoke when you are:

__ first getting up in the morning
__ in the bathroom
__ drinking coffee
__ arriving at work
__ typing
__ celebrating the completion of a project

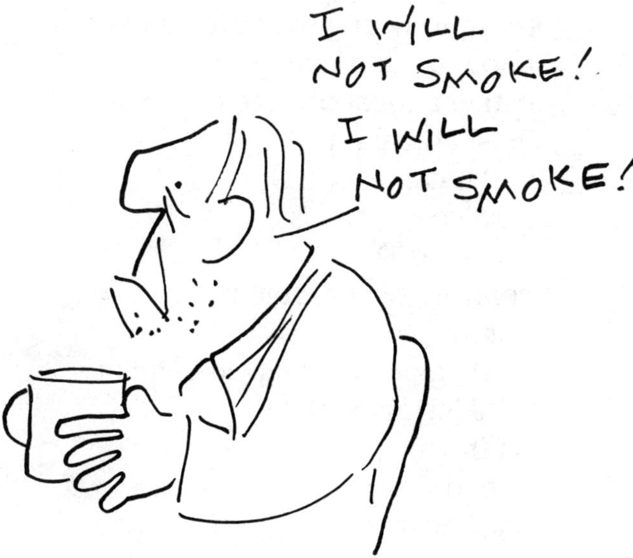
I WILL NOT SMOKE!
I WILL NOT SMOKE!

_ trying to stay calm
_ rewarding yourself
_ waiting
_ trying to keep your hands busy
_ about to start eating
_ eating a meal or snack
_ finished eating
_ in the car
_ reading
_ watching TV
_ confronting a problem
_ bored
_ reading or watching cigarette ads
_ drinking alcohol
_ on the telephone
_ in bed
_ finished sex
_ trying not to eat
_ at the intermission of a
  performance
_ leaving a performance/movie/
  sporting event
_ feeling tired
_ close to or see a cigarette
  package

Other triggers that lead me to smoke:

— _____

— _____

— _____

— _____

— _____

NOW you have identified the enemy but more important, you now know when he will strike. *You are prepared.*

10 ON YOUR MARK, GET SET, STOP

Think of it as training for a big race. If you don't prepare for it ahead of time, you might run out of steam before you reach the finish line.

It's the same when you set out to quit smoking. Before you start to kick the habit you need to give yourself the best chance for success. Here are a few pointers:

TREAT YOUR BODY WELL. It will have enough to go through. Give it sufficient sleep, plenty of exercise, and drink lots of water.

PICK A TIME TO QUIT SMOKING when you will be under the least possible stress. For example, don't try to quit when you're starting a new job. Let's not make this harder on you than it has to be.

GET SUPPORT. Ask two or three of your most supportive friends or family members to be there when you need encouragement or just an understanding ear.

INVOLVE OTHER PEOPLE. Make a bet with someone, have a friend sponsor you or, better yet, quit with someone else.

Think of those PEOPLE WHO MIGHT MAKE IT TOUGH FOR YOU TO QUIT.

Now how can you reduce their negative effects on you?

MAKE SMOKING INCONVENIENT. In the next chapter you'll be determining how many cigarettes you'll be smoking each day. Keep only that number of cigarettes on hand. Stop buying cigarettes by the carton. Buy only one pack at a time.

STOP SMOKING AUTOMATICALLY. Put your allotment of cigarettes for each day in an unfamiliar place (different pocket, another drawer) to break your automatic reach for them. Keep any others in an even more inconvenient spot.

THINK OF A CIGARETTE REPLACEMENT. When you need a pick-me-up try a sugarless candy, a stick of gum, popcorn, fruit, fruit juice or carrot stick instead. It might just do the trick.

MAKE SMOKING UNPLEASANT. Don't empty your ashtrays. Smoke in circumstances that are not particularly pleasant. Watch yourself in a mirror when you smoke. Focus on how you're killing yourself. Switch brands every time you buy cigarettes.

START A QUIT-SMOKING FUND. Set aside all the money you will be saving by smoking less and then by quitting. Plan something special to spend it on.

TAKE ONE DAY AT A TIME. It can be overwhelming to think about never smoking again. Just get through *this* craving and *this* day, and you'll be well on your way.

But most of all — REMEMBER THOSE YOU LOVE. Keep photos by your ash-trays of those you are killing with your second-hand smoke. Look at your cigarettes and then at your loved ones . . . and make the *smart* choice.

11 MEETING THE ENEMY HEAD ON

If you're like me you hate filling out forms. Trust me, this one is important. It's not necessary to bang your head against the fridge trying to come up with the right answer. Approximate numbers are just fine.

And if you're one of the diehard puffers who just can't start or finish the day without a cigarette between your lips DON'T DO IT. Smokers who can wait at least half an hour to light up after waking in the morning have a 97% chance of quitting.

At least let the statistics work *for* you.

Now let's get on with it and determine your new smoking schedule:

DAY 1

_____
(fill in date)

A) How many cigarettes do you smoke per day? _____

B) How many hours are you awake each day? _____

C) Because you will no longer be smoking during the half-hour after you wake up or the half-hour before you go to sleep, subtract one hour from your total in *B* _____

You now have the number of hours you have in which to smoke per day.

D) Multiply the total in *C* x 60 minutes

_____

DAY 3

———————————————

was smoking one cigarette
minutes.
g 5 minutes to that total,
smoke one cigarette every
tes.

DAY 4

———————————————

was smoking one cigarette
minutes.
g 5 minutes to that total,
smoke one cigarette every
tes.

DAY 5

———————————————

was smoking one cigarette
minutes.

... AND TO EXPLAIN THE PENALTIES FOR THOSE CAUGHT SMOKING IN THE WASHROOMS, HERE IS OUR OWN PEGGY 'THE CRUSHER' STYLES

This is the total number of minutes you have in which to smoke each day.

E) Divide *A*   (number of cigarettes) into *C* (number of minutes)

———

You now know the number of minutes that should pass between each cigarette you smoke per day.

For example:
A) I smoke 20 cigarettes a day.
B) I am awake 17 hours a day.
C) I now have 16 hours a day in which to smoke.
D) This equals 960 minutes a day in which to smoke.
E) I now know that I should smoke one cigarette every 48 minutes.

Now you know how many cigarettes you should smoke per day and the number of minutes between each ciga-

rette. Do
until you'
hour. Als
last cigar
before y

Now look
triggers y
Try to av
time you
situation
well as d
you must
logical de

On Day 1
every ___
After add
today I wi
___ min

On Day 2
every ___
After addi
today I wi
___ minu

On Day 3
every ___
After addi
today I wi
___ minu

On Day 4
every ___

After adding 5 minutes to that total, today I will smoke one cigarette every _____ minutes.

DAY 6

_____

On Day 5 I was smoking one cigarette every _____ minutes.
After adding 5 minutes to that total, today I will smoke one cigarette every _____ minutes.

DAY 7

_____

On Day 6 I was smoking one cigarette every _____ minutes.
After adding 5 minutes to that total, today I will smoke one cigarette every _____ minutes.

NOW, at the end of a week I am smoking only _____ cigarettes per day!

CONGRATULATIONS!!

How are you feeling now that you're well on your way to becoming a non-smoker? If you're a bit nervous or edgy don't worry. It's only natural.

BUT STAY WITH THE PROGRAM.

Need some reminders why you're quitting? Let's go over them again:

* you are a junkie
* smoking is expensive
* it's anti-social
* it's killing you
* and you're taking your loved ones with you!

12 DIGGING IN

You're already on your way. Aren't you proud of yourself?

Remind yourself where you were a week ago — *look what you've already achieved!*

Unlike Rocky Balboa, you might not yet be in shape to run up a long flight of stairs and shadow box at the top. Who is?

But what your body has noticed is that the usual influx of poisons had dropped off. Your system is beginning to adjust to a lower level of nicotine.

You're also separating the act of smoking from your trigger situations. Your psychological addiction is also lessening.

Take a deep breath of fresh air. Let your lungs know that this is only the beginning.

Continue on the same program as last week, increasing your time between cigarettes by five minutes each day. Remember to try to avoid lighting up while you're experiencing a trigger situation.

FRESH AIR

This is the total number of minutes you have in which to smoke each day.

E) Divide *A* (number of cigarettes) into *C* (number of minutes)

———

You now know the number of minutes that should pass between each cigarette you smoke per day.

For example:
A) I smoke <u>20</u> cigarettes a day.
B) I am awake <u>17</u> hours a day.
C) I now have <u>16</u> hours a day in which to smoke.
D) This equals <u>960</u> minutes a day in which to smoke.
E) I now know that I should smoke one cigarette every <u>48</u> minutes.

Now you know how many cigarettes you should smoke per day and the number of minutes between each cigarette. Don't begin your *first* cigarette until you've been awake for *half an hour*. Also, be sure you finish your *last* cigarette of the day *half an hour* before you go to bed.

Now look back at chapter nine. What triggers you to light up a cigarette? Try to avoid smoking at the same time you are experiencing a trigger situation. This is very important. As well as defeating your drug addiction you must also overcome your psychological dependence on tobacco.

DAY 2

_____

On Day 1 I was smoking one cigarette every _____ minutes.
After adding 5 minutes to that total, today I will smoke one cigarette every _____ minutes.

DAY 3

_____

On Day 2 I was smoking one cigarette
every _____ minutes.
After adding 5 minutes to that total,
today I will smoke one cigarette every
_____ minutes.

DAY 4

_____

On Day 3 I was smoking one cigarette
every _____ minutes.
After adding 5 minutes to that total,
today I will smoke one cigarette every
_____ minutes.

DAY 5

_____

On Day 4 I was smoking one cigarette
every _____ minutes.

After adding 5 minutes to that total, today I will smoke one cigarette every _____ minutes.

DAY 6

_____

On Day 5 I was smoking one cigarette every _____ minutes.
After adding 5 minutes to that total, today I will smoke one cigarette every _____ minutes.

DAY 7

_____

On Day 6 I was smoking one cigarette every _____ minutes.
After adding 5 minutes to that total, today I will smoke one cigarette every _____ minutes.

NOW, at the end of a week I am smoking only _____ cigarettes per day!

CONGRATULATIONS!!

How are you feeling now that you're well on your way to becoming a non-smoker? If you're a bit nervous or edgy don't worry. It's only natural.

BUT STAY WITH THE PROGRAM.

Need some reminders why you're quit-ting? Let's go over them again:

* you are a junkie
* smoking is expensive
* it's anti-social
* it's killing you
* and you're taking your loved ones with you!

12 DIGGING IN

You're already on your way. Aren't you proud of yourself?

Remind yourself where you were a week ago — *look what you've already achieved!*

Unlike Rocky Balboa, you might not yet be in shape to run up a long flight of stairs and shadow box at the top. Who is?

But what your body has noticed is that the usual influx of poisons had dropped off. Your system is beginning to adjust to a lower level of nicotine.

You're also separating the act of smoking from your trigger situations. Your psychological addiction is also lessening.

Take a deep breath of fresh air. Let your lungs know that this is only the beginning.

Continue on the same program as last week, increasing your time between cigarettes by five minutes each day. Remember to try to avoid lighting up while you're experiencing a trigger situation.

FRESH
AIR

When you've cut down to about seven cigarettes a day you can quit cold turkey. Or continue reducing each day if you feel you're not ready to take the plunge.

WEEK TWO

DAY 8, _____ :
                    (fill in date)
I will smoke 1 cigarette every _____ minutes.

DAY 9, _____ :
I will smoke 1 cigarette every _____ minutes.

DAY 10, _____ :
I will smoke 1 cigarette every _____ minutes.

DAY 11, _____ :
I will smoke 1 cigarette every _____ minutes.

DAY 12, _____ :
I will smoke 1 cigarette every _____ minutes.

DAY 13, _____ :
I will smoke 1 cigarette every _____
minutes.

DAY 14, _____ :
I will smoke 1 cigarette every _____
minutes.

WEEK THREE

DAY 15, _____ :
I will smoke 1 cigarette every _____
minutes.

DAY 16, _____ :
I will smoke 1 cigarette every _____
minutes.

DAY 17, _____ :
I will smoke 1 cigarette every _____
minutes.

DAY 18, _____ :
I will smoke 1 cigarette every _____
minutes.

DAY 19, _____:
I will smoke 1 cigarette every _____
minutes.

DAY 20, _____:
I will smoke 1 cigarette every _____
minutes.

DAY 21, _____:
I will smoke 1 cigarette every _____
minutes.

By now some of you will already be non-
smokers!

As a non-smoker you have increased
your life span — you will *not* be amongst
the ranks of the three million people who
will die this year as a result of smoking.

Your second-hand smoke will no longer
endanger the lives of the ones you love.

Your food will begin to taste better, your
sense of smell is returning . . . and think
of the money you've already saved!

WEEK FOUR

DAY 22,_____:
I will smoke 1 cigarette every _____
minutes.

DAY 23, _____:
I will smoke 1 cigarette every _____
minutes.

DAY 24, _____:
I will smoke 1 cigarette every _____
minutes.

DAY 25, _____:
I will smoke 1 cigarette every _____
minutes.

DAY 26, _____:
I will smoke 1 cigarette every _____
minutes.

DAY 27, _____:
I will smoke 1 cigarette every _____
minutes.

DAY 28, _____:
I will smoke 1 cigarette every _____
minutes.

WEEK FIVE

DAY 29, _____:
I will smoke 1 cigarette every _____
minutes.

DAY 30, _____:
I will smoke 1 cigarette every _____
minutes.

DAY 31, _____:
I will smoke 1 cigarette every _____
minutes.

DAY 32, _____:
I will smoke 1 cigarette every _____
minutes.

DAY 33, _____:
I will smoke 1 cigarette every _____
minutes.

DAY 34, _____:
I will smoke 1 cigarette every _____
minutes.

DAY 35, _____:
I will smoke 1 cigarette every _____
minutes.

WEEK SIX

DAY 36, _____:
I will smoke 1 cigarette every _____
minutes.

DAY 37, _____:
I will smoke 1 cigarette every _____
minutes.

DAY 38, _____:
I will smoke 1 cigarette every _____
minutes.

DAY 39, _____:
I will smoke 1 cigarette every _____
minutes.

DAY 40, _____:
I will smoke 1 cigarette every _____
minutes.

DAY 41, _____:
I will smoke 1 cigarette every _____
minutes.

DAY 42, _____:
I will smoke 1 cigarette every _____
minutes.

For those of you who have yet to taper off to being non-smokers, continue with this program of adding five minutes to your time between cigarettes each day. Remember, when you're smoking seven cigarettes a day or less you should consider quitting altogether.

YOU'VE KICKED THE HABIT... NO, HOLD IT! YES... NO... YOU'VE STARTED SMOKING AGAIN

13 AND YOU THOUGHT YOU COULDN'T DO IT

How about that! You're now a non-smoker.

But before you step up to get your medal, look over your shoulder. At this early stage there are all manner of temptations waiting to lure you back to the smoking and choking brigade.

Remember, there is a tremendous danger that you will be tempted to smoke just one cigarette during a time of stress or during one of your trigger situations.

Most of those who fall back into the smoking trap do so during their first week of quitting. Your body is saying, "What the hell is going on? Where is the poison you've been feeding me?"

Let's face it. Changes are taking place. You're about to get back to feeling fit. But be careful. You're still going through a vulnerable period. Just hold on for three months and the worst will be over.

And one other thing. If you do find yourself falling off the wagon, don't lose heart. Just climb back on again.

A RELAPSE DOESN'T MEAN FAILURE. It often takes several attempts to break the habit.

Use all the resources at your disposal to help you. Review the reasons you want to quit, visualize life without addiction, employ any helpful hints and seek out sympathetic family members or friends.

You already know what situations trigger you. Anticipate them and know that they will continue to tempt you to smoke. Think of ways to cope with these situations without cigarettes.

When you really feel in need of a nicotine fix, muster up all your willpower and keep yourself busy for five minutes. The craving will pass.

Play with something to keep your hands busy, like a marble, worry beads, a pencil.

Do the same for your mouth. Although it might not look too appealing, try sucking on a toothpick or straw to soothe your mouth during times of temptation. And remember, sugarless candies or gum will also help.

And for heavens sake stop worrying about putting on weight! JUST BECAUSE YOU QUIT SMOKING DOESN'T MEAN YOU'RE GOING TO GET FAT. You'll only gain weight if you replace cigarettes with the wrong foods.

YOU'RE THE SAME AS LAST WEEK

Get rid of that stench of tobacco around the house. Have all your clothes cleaned, even buy flowers as often as you can. Climb out of your reeking ashtray and breathe in the new, fresh air. Now, who would want to stink up your sweet-smelling home?

Visit a dentist and have your teeth cleaned. Brush your teeth frequently and after meals to maintain sparkling-fresh breath.

Throw away your cigarettes, matches, lighters and ashtrays.

Try to keep busy. See a movie, go for walks, start a hobby. Just make it something you enjoy and find relaxing. What you don't need is more stress in your life.

Avoid dangerous situations — places where everyone else seems to be smoking. Sit in the non-smoking section of a restaurant. Try to travel on non-smoking flights; if not, sit in the non-smoking section.

If you're tempted to smoke when you drive, tape your ashtray shut and take your lighter out of the car.

Associate more with non-smokers and try to socialize in smoke-free environments.

Exercise more. As well as being good for you, it's hard to imagine smoking while you're swimming, jogging or playing tennis!

Determine some relaxation techniques that work for you. Exercise might do the trick, or perhaps you'd rather soak in a hot tub or meditate.

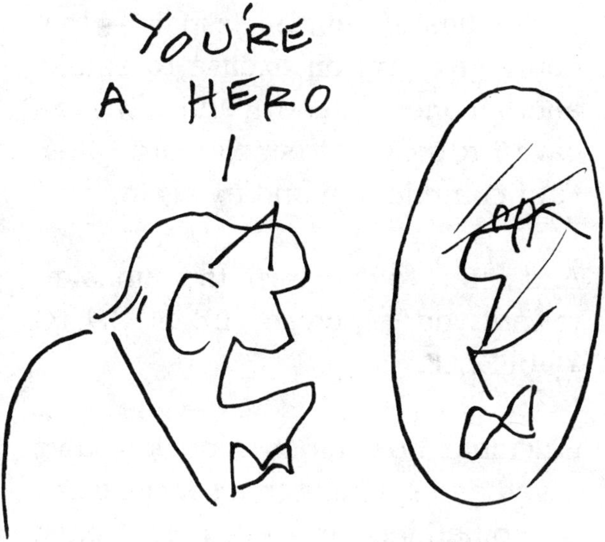
YOU'RE
A HERO

Avoid caffeine and get lots of rest.

If you give in to the temptation and light up that first cigarette, don't give in to feelings of guilt or despair — that could give you an excuse to smoke another one. Instead, identify why you gave in to the urge to smoke, strengthen your commitment and try again.

And after you've beat the monster, reward your progress. BE GOOD TO YOURSELF.

Calculate how much money you've saved and spend it on a special treat. Do something fun to celebrate each week or month without cigarettes (or maybe after just one particularly grueling day).

One friend and her husband quit smoking together and keep putting aside the

money they would have spent on cigarettes. Once a month they take these
savings and have a glorious night on
the town.

Another couple took a trip to Greece
after a year of smoker's savings.

But you don't need me to tell you how
to spend your money. Just have fun
and enjoy feeling great!

CONCLUSION

I'd like to say that if, after reading this book, you are still a smoker I will return the money you paid for it. But I won't.

If you *have* finally stopped smoking because of my help, that's fantastic!

So have a long and happy life. And when you make out your will, remember good and faithful Ben — without who's help you'd have spent a hell of a lot shorter time on this earth.

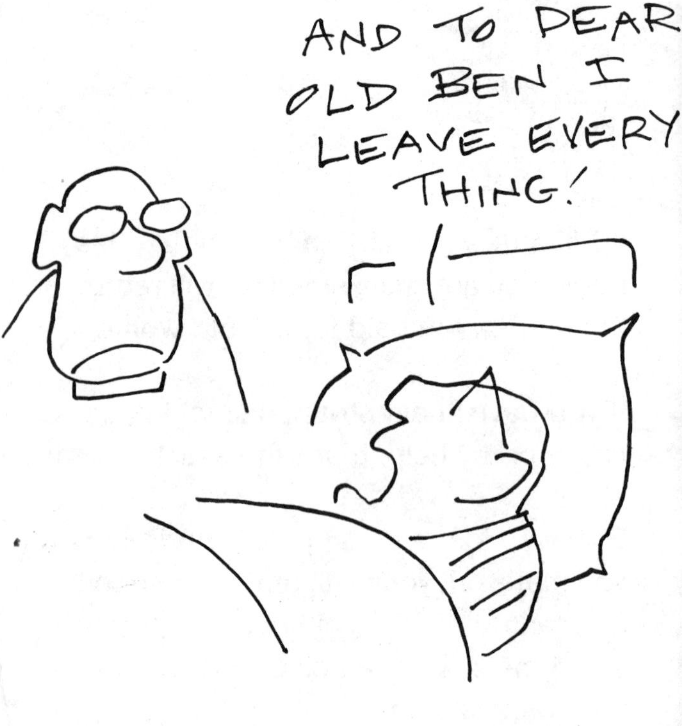
AND TO DEAR OLD BEN I LEAVE EVERY THING!